The Best

What Am I Riddles

300 RIDDLES, BRAINTEASERS AND PUZZLES FOR THE WHOLE FAMILY

M. PREFONTAINE

i

INTRODUCTION

This is a fun book of 300 traditional 'What am I?' riddles for the whole family.

They are designed to test logic, lateral thinking as well as memory and to engage the brain in seeing patterns and connections between different things and circumstances.

The book is split into four chapters graduating in difficulty, in the view of the author, as you move through the book.

If all else fails, the answers are at the back of the book.

CONTENTS

EASY

1. 100 feet in the air but back on the ground.
What am I?

2. I have eight to spare and I am covered in hair.
What am I?

3. I have no fingers, but I can still point. I have no arms, but I can still strike. I have no feet, but I can still run.
What am I?

4. I can be used to build castles, but I crumble in your hands. I can help you to see and I am found all around the lands.
What am I?

5. You heard me once, and then again. Afterwards I fade away, until you call me again.
What am I?

6. Sometimes I can run but do not walk. Wherever I go you will follow close behind.
What am I?

7. Everyone needs me and wants me, yet everyone gives me away every day.
What am I?

8. You can only use me when I am broken.
What am I?

9. I have many rings and get a brand new one every year, but they are not worth much. They will tell you how old I am.
What am I?

10. Kings and queens may cling to power, and the jesters may have their call. However, I can defeat them all.
What am I?

11. Everyone always overlooks me but everyone has me.
What am I?

12. I am a time of year for gathering crops. Remove the first three letters I become something you can wear.
What am I?

13. I only exist when you are here. Where you never were, I can never be.
What am I?

14. I have a head and I have a tail, but my eyes can never see my tail.
What am I?

15. I arrive at night without being fetched. I hide away as soon as daylight comes. I may look small, but I am much mightier than you can imagine.
What am I?

16. I am lighter than what I am made of. You can see a part of me but more of me is hidden underneath.
What am I?

17. I cannot be stolen, but I can be given out. I am owned by all, those with too little will have doubts.
What am I?

18. I am a fruit with seed on the outside.
What am I?

19. I am clean when I'm black, dirty when I'm white.
What am I?

20. I have wheels and flies, yet I am not an aircraft.
What am I?

21. I can speak but have a metal tongue. I cannot breathe, for I have no lung.
What am I?

22. I have two eyes in my head and many eyes on my tail.
What am I?

23. The faster you run, the harder it is to catch me.
What am I?

24. Though I am only two words, I have thousands of letters in me.
What am I?

25. The more of me there is, the less you see.
What am I?

26. I am a kind of cheese which is made backwards.
What am I?

27. I work when I play and play when I work.
What am I?

28. I have thirteen hearts but don't have a body or a soul.
What am I?

29. I am drawn by everyone without pen or pencil.
What am I?

30. I am the only vegetable or fruit that is never sold frozen, canned, processed, or in any other form but fresh.
What am I?

31. I can fill a room but will take up no space.
What am I?

32. I smell like blue paint, pour like green paint, but I look like a red truck.
What am I?

33. I am the type of room you cannot enter or leave. I rise from the ground below. I could be poisonous.
What am I?

34. I jump when I walk and sit when I stand.
What am I?

35. As a state in America. I am round on both sides and high in the middle.
What am I?

36. I am invisible, I cannot be seen, weigh nothing, and if you put me in a barrel, it will become lighter.
What am I?

37. I am a ring, but I am square.
What am I?

38. I am heavy forward, but backward I'm not.
What am I?

39. You can use me but can't touch me.
What am I?

40. You can hold me in your left hand but not your right.
What am I?

41. I am an ancient invention that allows people to see through walls.
What am I?

42. I can go up and down without moving.
What am I?

43. Until I am measured, I am not known.
Yet how you miss me when I have flown.
What am I?

44. I tie two people together but touch only one.
What am I?

45. I am always coming but never arrive.
What am I?

46. I drape the hills in white, I do not swallow, but I do bite.
What am I?

47. I am an instrument that you can hear, but you cannot touch or see me.
What am I?

48. I have a foot but no leg.
What am I?

49. I grow when I eat but die when I drink.
What am I?

50. I have teeth but cannot bite.
What am I?

51. You can catch me, but you cannot throw me anywhere.
What am I?

52. I am the next letter in the letter sequence:-
ottffssen.
What am I?

53. I am within you and can be said to be broken without being touched.
What am I?

54. If you remove some from me you will cause trouble.
What am I?

55. I am a number, but I am countless. I am compared with other things, but nothing compares to me.
What am I?

56. On the outside, I have beige walls which surround a castle of the purest white, and a treasure of liquid gold hides in the center.
What am I?

57. I don't exist but have a name.
What am I?

58. I have seven colours, but there is no gold.
What am I?

59. I am as old as the earth, but I am renewed every month.
What am I?

60. You have one, but others use yours more than you do.
What is it?

61. I always go to bed with my shoes on.
What am I?

62. I am in the middle of water but I am not an island.
What am I?

63. I am an ant that is good at math.
What am I?

64. I am called a celebrity fish, but I am neither.
What am I?

65. I help engines to turn and can help your trousers to stay up.
What am I?

66. My voice is tender, my waist is slender and I am often invited to play. Yet wherever I go I must take my bow otherwise I have nothing to say.
What am I?

67. The eight of us go forth to protect our king from the enemy's attack.
What am I?

68. I am an animal as well as a hair product.
What am I?

69. U always follow me and I am rare.
What am I?

70. I can be cracked, made, told and played.
What am I?

71. Tear me off and scratch my head.
What was once red is now black.
What am I?

72. I begin with a T and end with a T. T is also within me.
What am I?

73. I am the building with the most stories.
What am I?

74. There is one in every corner and two in every room.
What am I?

75. I am higher than a king.
What am I?

MEDIUM

1. I'm lighter than a feather, yet the strongest man can't hold me for more than 5 minutes.
What am I?

2. I am the beginning of the end, the end of every place. I am the beginning of eternity, the end of time and space.
What am I?

3. The more holes that you cover the lower I will go.
What am I?

4. You use me from your head to your toes, the more I do the less of me remains.
What am I?

5. I will always run but never walk, often murmur but never talk I have a bed but never sleep and have a mouth but never eat.
What am I?

6. I go through a door but never go in and never come out.
What am I?

7. I am pronounced as one letter, written with three. I come in blue, black, brown, or grey. Reverse me and I read the same either way.
What am I?

8. My clothes come off when you put on your clothes. However, I get them back when you take your clothes off.
What am I?

9. I do lots of work but only when there is something in my eye.
What am I?

10. I fly away as soon as you set me loose. People around you may slowly move away once they sense my presence.
What am I?

11. I sleep when you are awake, I am awake when you fall asleep. I can fly but have no feathers to aid my flight.
What am I?

12. I am all around you, but you cannot see me. I have no throat but can roar. I am welcomed during the summer but despised in the winter.
 What am I?

13. I love to twist and dance. I have no wings, but I fly high up into the sky.
What am I?

14. You throw me out when you use me and take me in when you are done.
What am I?

15. I am gold and can be black and white, I'm a symbol for a nation, when freedom took flight.
What am I?

16. I provide light, yet I am solid. Without me you would feel enclosed. I do not like being touched, especially with a lot of force. I like to be in buildings.
What am I?

17. I am an unruly field that reaches far. Yet I have no tracks and am crossed without paths.
What am I?

18. My tail is long, my coat is brown, I like the country, I like the town. I can live in a house or live in a shed, And I come out to play when you are in bed.
What am I?

19. I am the word that has three syllables and twenty six letters.
What am I?

20. Six legs, two heads, two hands, one long nose. Yet I use only four legs wherever I go.
What am I?

21. I'm not a bird, but I can fly through the sky. I'm not a river, but I'm full of water.
What am I?

22. I am a drum which beats a sound without being touched, and once I am silent it will be the death of you.
What am I?

23. Brothers and sisters, have I none, but this man's father is my father's son.
Who is he?

24. I am the kind of nut that is empty at the center and have no shell. No plant will ever grow from me.
What am I?

25. I have three feet but no arms or legs.
What am I?

26. I bring light to a murky world. In a current I travel and through tunnels I run. However, if you touch me, then I can kill you.
What am I?

27. I am gentle enough to soothe your skin, light enough to fly in the sky, strong enough to crack rocks.
What am I?

28. I am a seed with three letters in my name. Take away the last two and I still sound the same.
What am I?

29. I am a word. I become longer when the third letter is removed.
What am I?

30. I have no eyes and no legs. I have no ears and I am strong enough to move the earth.
What am I?

31. I only point in one direction, but I guide people around the world.
What am I?

32. I am higher without a head than with one.
What am I?

33. A man shaves several times a day, yet he still has a beard.
Who is this man?

34. You are my brother, but I am not your brother.
Who am I?

35. I am a key that can open a banana.
What am I?

36. There are 5 small items used every day you'll find in 'a Tennis Court'.
What are they?

37. I have four wings, but cannot fly, I never laugh and never cry; on the same spot I'm always found, toiling away with little sound.
What am I?

38. I have a tongue but cannot taste. I have a soul but cannot feel.
What am I?

39. I have an eye but cannot see. I'm faster than any man alive yet have no limbs.
What am I?

40. You can swallow me but I can also swallow you up as well.
What am I?

41. I stay where I am even when I go off.
What am I?

42. You wear me every day but you never put me on. I will change colors if you leave me outside too long.
What am I?

43. I demand an answer but don't ask a question.
What am I?

44. I have ten letters and start with gas.
What am I?

45. I cannot hear or even see, but sense light and sounds that there may be. Sometimes I end up on the hook, or even deep into a book.
What am I?

46. I taste better than I smell.
What am I?

47. I am bought by the yard and worn by the foot.
What am I?

48. I am two. Without one or the other both would not exist.
What am I?

49. I have no end, beginning or middle.
What am I?

50. I can be served but not eaten.
What am I?

51. I have a trunk but I am not an elephant. I have a bark but I am not a dog. I am made from fresh air.
What am I?

52. I am a little house full of food but no door to go in.
What am I?

53. I am always found two in a coffin. I love to start a fight, and two of me make a difference.
What am I?

54. I am found in man and I can be found in animals. I can also be found in the City Liverpool, yet not in plants.
What am I?

55. I am a Roman God and a speck of rust in the night sky.
Who am I?

56. I can hurt without moving and poison without touching. I bear both truth and lies and am not judged by our size.
What am I?

57. I wear a red coat and have a stone in my throat.
What am I?

58. I go up to empty my load, and then return down again.
What am I?

59. I drive away my customers, but they are still happy to pay me.
What am I?

60. I am a cold man without a soul. If there is warmth in me it will slowly destroy me.
What am I?

61. My teeth are sharp, and my back is straight, to cut things up is my fate.
What am I?

62. I am not a bird, but I can fly through the sky. I am not a river but am full of water.
What am I?

63. I am at the head of an elephant and the tail of a squirrel.
What am I?

64. Every dawn begins with me and at dusk I will be the first you see. Daybreak couldn't come without me.
What am I?

65. I have a frame but no pictures. I have two poles, but they are lying flat.
What am I?

66. I am sometimes light and sometimes dark and swim amongst the twinkling lights. Seas and oceans obey me but mountains I cannot move.
What am I?

67. I like to twirl my body but keep my head up high. After I go in everything becomes tight.
What am I?

68. I can be long or short. I can be grown or bought. I can be painted or left bare. What am I?

69. I am white and perfect for cutting and grinding. I am a useful tool for most mammals.
What am I?

70. I have a neck but no head.
What am I?

71. I never was but always will be. No one ever saw me, but everyone knows I exist.
What am I?

72. I row quickly with four oars yet never come out from under my roof. What am I?

73. Glittering points that downward thrust. Sparkling spears that never rust. What am I?

74. People buy me to eat but never eat me.
What am I?

75. I am the number you get when you multiply all the numbers on a telephone together.
What am I?

DIFFICULT

1. You throw away my outside and then eat what is inside. Then you throw away the inside.
What am I?

2. I only weigh about 3lbs but have given myself a name.
What am I?

3. I am black, but light can be shone on me. Different lights will make me change size.
What am I?

4. I am soft and hairy from door to door. I am the pet that always stays in the house and on the floor.
What am I?

5. I am a coat, but you can only put me on when I am wet.
What am I?

6. As I get hotter I get bigger and climb ever higher. However, I can never escape from my glass prison.
What am I?

7. I open my jaws when you poke two fingers in me. I especially like to devour papers.
What am I?

8. I am an insect, but within me is another insect. I am the misspelt name of a famous band.
What am I?

9. You cannot keep me until you have given me to someone else.
What am I?

10. When you see me at work I am blue, but when you see me at rest I'm red. You don't see me too often. I'm there for you if you're hurt, but I'm vital for you if you are hurt or not.
What am I?

11. You can throw me off from the highest building and I won't break, but I will break if you place me in water.
What am I?

12. I am a box who holds keys but not locks. With the right combination of keys, I may unlock your soul.
What am I?

13. H,I,J,K,L,M,N,O
What am I?

14. I can be driven but have no wheels. I can be sliced but remain whole.
What am I?

15. I am wooden, but I am neither hard, straight, or crooked.
What am I?

16. I can go right through a pane of glass without breaking it.
What am I?

17. I can be repeated but rarely in the same way. I can't be changed but can be rewritten. I can be passed down but should not be forgotten.
What am I?

18. I have many wheels but move I do not. Call me what I am, call me a lot.
What am I?

19. You can see but not hear me.
What am I?

20. I turn around once. What is out will not get in. I turn around again. What is in will not get out.
What am I?

21. Weight in my belly, trees on my back, nails in my ribs, feet I do lack.
What am I?

22. I have no head, and a tail I lack, but I do have arms, and legs, and back; I inhabit the palace, the tavern, the cot, 'tis a beggarly residence where I am not.
What am I?

23. I wiggle and cannot see, sometimes underground and sometimes in a tree. I really don't want to be on a hook, and I become a person when combined with book.
What am I?

24. With three eyes and as black as night, I frequently knock down ten men with a single strike.
What am I?

25. I'm the part of the bird that's not in the sky. I can swim in the ocean and yet remain dry.
What am I?

26. I fly without wings and I cry without eyes.
What am I?

27. I am easy to lift but hard to throw?
What am I?

28. I am full of holes but still hold water.
What am I?

29. The first two letters of an English word refer to a man, the first three refer to a woman, the first four to a great man and the whole word to a great woman. What am I?

30. Turn me on my side and I am everything. Cut me in half and I am nothing.
What am I?

31. I move slowly but I'm dead. I leave and then I'm back. I'm clear and then I'm red. I'm many neurotics' snack.
What am I?

32. With pointed fangs I sit and wait, with piercing force I serve out fate. Grabbing bloodless victims, proclaiming my might, physically joining with a single bite.
What am I?

33. I grow up and down at the same time. What am I?

34. Countless blades that do not cut but am cut by kids to make a buck. What am I?

35. Late afternoons I often bathe. I'll soak in water piping hot. My essence goes through my see-through clothes. Used up I've gone to pot. What am I?

36. I have a long neck, a name of a bird and feed on cargo of ships. I am not alive. What am I?

37. If you eat me my sender will eat you. What am I?

38. A three-letter word I'm sure you know, I can be on a boat or a sleigh in the snow, I'm pals with the rain and honor a king, but my favorite use is attached to a string.
What am I?

39. Although I'm far from the point, I'm not a mistake. I fix yours.
What am I?

40. No matter how much rain falls I won't get any wetter.
What am I?

41. I stare at you, you stare at me. I have three eyes yet can't see. Every time I blink, I give you commands. You do as you are told, with your feet and hands.
What am I?

42. I am a sport that starts with a T, has four letters, and is played around the world.
What am I?

43. You can easily touch me, but not see me. You can throw me out, but not away.
What am I?

44. I get dirty in about 5 days but it takes 5 minutes to clean me. It takes a long time for me to be long but I can be short in 5 seconds.
What am I?

45. You like to kill me but in the end, I kill you.
What am I?

46. I can't go left, I can't go right. I am forever stuck in a building over three stories high.
What am I?

47. People look at me all the time. I have a large vocabulary. I can teach people a lot of new things. I can be mysterious, funny, adventurous, romantic, scary, and sad. I tell stories. I can take people to other worlds.
What am I?

48. I can hurt you, but you cannot touch me.
What am I?

49. I don't have eyes, but once I did see. Once I had thoughts, but now I'm white and empty.
What am I?

50. Whoever makes it, tells it not. Whoever takes it, knows it not. And whoever knows it wants it not.
What am I?

51. I fly after I am first born, but then will lie down. After I die I will run away. What am I?

52. I am a letter but am nowhere in the periodic table.
What am I?

53. My scales do not weigh grams, ounces or pounds. However, I can provide food for the soul.
What am I?

54. I am long, thin and twisting but can turn one story into another.
What am I?

55. I am a heavy seven letter word. If you take away two you are left with eight.
What am I?

56. I am a house that will last far longer than any mason, builder or carpenter will build.
What am I?

57. You put me in dry and I get wet. The longer I stay in the stronger it will get.
What am I?

58. My blades are slashed by another's blades, but I lie low to survive. I am busiest during the summer.
What am I?

59. I have cold head and feet and am as round as a ball. I am always turning on myself.
What am I?

60. I am an old relative who's hands can't hold anything and who's eyes can't see anything.
What am I?

61. I make things short, but I am pretty long myself.
What am I?

62. I may only be given but never bought. Sinners seek me, but saints do not
What am I?

63. When I get closer my tail gets longer, but as I move away my tail leads the way.
What am I?

64. I am an open-ended barrel and am shaped like a hive. I am filled with flesh but my work is so so.
What am I?

65. I am a word that is pluralized by adding the letter C.
What am I?

66. I soar without any wings, I see without eyes. I have traveled the universe and conquered the world yet never left home.
What am I?

67. I am a band but don't perform, sing or act.
What am I?

68. I go inside boots but outside shoes.
What am I?

69. A golden treasure I contain which is guarded by thousands. Stored in a labyrinth where no man walks, yet men often steal my gold.
What am I?

70. Draw, fire or drill me I am always empty.
What am I?

71. I sound like a colorful fish, but that is just a distraction.
What am I?

72. When I am angry I turn red. When cold I turn blue and white when scared.
What am I?

73. Large as a mountain, small as a pea, endlessly swimming in a waterless sea.
What am I?

74. I am a language that people speak without uttering a word.
What am I?

75. Too much for one, enough for two, but nothing for three.
What am I?

FIENDISH

1. When I am skinny I am fast, but when I am fat I am slow, but I'll still delight you from your eyes to your nose.
What am I?

2. Thirty men and only two women, but the women are the strongest. They are all dressed in black or white and they can fight for hours.
What am I?

3. I have a name, but it is not mine, and no one cares about me in their prime. People cry at my sight and lie by me all day and night.
What am I?

4. I go up and I go down, towards the sky and the ground. I'm present and past tense too. Let's go for a ride, me and you.
What am I?

5. I have a ring but no fingers. I used to stay still all the time, but nowadays I follow you around.
What am I?

6. I am alive but am without breath and cold as death. I am never thirsty but drink continuously to live.
What am I?

7. I go from town to town and house to house. Whether it rains or snows I will sleep outside at night.
What am I?

8. I have cities but have no people, forests but no trees, and oceans with no water.
What am I?

9. I have fingers and a pair of thumbs. However, I do not have flesh, feather, or scales.
What am I?

10. Sometimes I fly as fast as the speed of light. Sometimes I can crawl as slow as a snail. You will certainly miss me when I'm gone.
What am I?

11. I am a rock group with four members. All dead and one was assassinated.
What am I?

12. I am a food with 5 letters. If you remove the first letter I am a form of energy. Remove two and I'm needed to live. Scramble the last 3 and you can drink me down.
What am I?

13. I have a hundred legs, but cannot stand. I have a long neck, but no head. I cannot see, but I help keep your house neat and tidy.
What am I?

14. I can hiss like bacon frying. I am made with an egg, I have plenty of backbone, but lack a good leg. I peel layers like onions. I can be long, like a flagpole, yet fit in a hole.
What am I?

15. I'm as simple as a circle but worthless as a leader. When I follow a group, their strength increases tenfold. By myself I'm practically nothing.
What am I?

16. I dig out tiny caves, and store gold and silver in them. I also build bridges of silver and make crowns of gold. Sooner or later everybody needs my help, yet many people afraid to let me help them.
What am I?

17. I have long legs, crooked thighs, little head, and no eyes.
What am I?

18. My top and bottom both equal are, my waist is as slender as a bee's. Whether I stand on my head or my base I am quite the same. But if my head should be cut off I to nothing change.
What am I?

19. I am a three-letter word when I am single. Add a 'c' and I become more than one.
What am I?

20. The shorter I am, the bigger I am. What am I?

21. I am your father's sister's sister-in-law.
Who am I?

22. When I take five and add six. I get eleven, but when I take six and add seven, I get one.
What am I?

23. I open to close but I close to open. I'm surrounded by water but I'm never soaking.
What am I?

24. I have a neck and no head, two arms but no hands. I'm with you to school, I'm with you to work.
What am I?

25. I have three eyes and only one leg. Obey me or you will be sorry.
What am I?

26. I have two legs and they only touch the ground when I am not moving.
What am I?

27. I am a sport in which the winners move backwards, and the losers move forward.
What am I?

28. You go in through one hole, you come out through three holes. Once you're inside you're ready to go outside, but once you're outside you're still inside.
What am I?

29. There is a green house. Inside the green house, there is a white house. Inside the white house, there is a red house. Inside the red house, there are lots of babies.
Who am I?

30. In my core I have 5. But 500 stand in the beginning and the end of mine. I also include the first letter and the first number to make me complete. I am the name of a King.
Who am I?

31. I am a ten-letter word that can be created using only the top row of letters on a typewriter.
What am I?

32. I am a word that contains all 5 vowels.
What am I?

33. I am a house and has post on top, a roof at the bottom, while the rainwater comes from below.
What I am?

34. When the day after tomorrow is yesterday, today will be as far from Wednesday as today was from Wednesday when the day before yesterday was tomorrow.
What day is tomorrow?

35.
16, 06, 68, 88, ?, 98

What number replaces the question mark?

36. I am the ruler of shovels, I have a double, I am as thin as a knife, I also have a wife.
What am I?

37. My thunder comes before my lightning. My lightning comes before my rain. And my rain dries all the ground it touches.
What am I?

38. I can bring tears to your eyes; resurrect the dead, make you smile, and reverse time. I form in an instant but I last a life time.
What am I?

39. There are many different kinds but the one you pick doesn't do its job.
What am I?

40. If you throw me out of the window, I'll leave a grieving wife. Bring me back, but through a door, you'll see someone giving life.
What am I?

41. I am something, a lot of people don't like me, including you,but I'm called upon anytime one is injured. I like playing with pregnant women, I'm a 5 letter word, and if my last letter is put before first letter, I become a name of a country.
What am I?

42. I'm made up of 12 completely different letters, but you can type me with just 1.
What am I?

43. I am a fruit. You cross off the first letter I am a crime. Cross of the second letter I'm an animal. Cross off the next two letters I am a vowel.
What am I?

44. I have an eye but cannot see, take time to generate, and can dissipate in seconds.
What am I?

45. I go back and forth constantly but never in a straight line.
What am I?

46. I have 6 faces and 21 eyes but can't see a thing.
What am I?

47. I sit high glowing and watch the world go by, without me everything would seem dull and dangerous.
What am I?

48. Only one color, but not one size, stuck at the bottom, yet easily flies, present in sun, but not in rain, doing no harm, and feeling no pain.
What am I?

49. XLR8
What word am I?

50. I am in the eye of someone holding a bee.
What am I?

51. As a whole, I am both safe and secure. Behead me, and I become a place of meeting. Behead me again, and I am the partner of ready. Restore me, and I become the domain of beasts.
 What am I?

52. I am an English word of six letters. The last three letters are the past tense of its first three letters.
What am I?

53. I am a 5 letter word which when printed in capitals can be read the same upside down.
What am I?

54. I am made of wood but cannot be sawed.
What am I?

55. I am a smooth dance, a place to stay, an Asian Country and a girl's name.
What am I?

56. I am not a pool but have a cover. I am not a tree but I have leaves. I am not a shirt but have sleeves. I am not slave but am bound.
What am I?

57. I have weight in my stomach, trees are my back and nails in my ribs. However, I have no feet.
What am I?

58. I am three words that sound the same. One you can smell, one is delivered and the last you can spend.
What am I?

59. I am crucified to stop a murder.
What am I?

60. I have two meanings. One is to be broken and the other is to hold on.
What am I?

61. My first two letters say my name and my last asks a question. What I embrace I destroy eventually.
What am I?

62. I have two bodies which are joined together as one. When I stand still I run and run.
What am I?

63. My first half is a waste container, and my whole is a language that few understand.
What am I?

64. With a halo of water and a tongue of wood. A body of stone has long stood. What am I?

65. My head bobs lazily in your lawn. Many think I am cute with my face of yellow and hair of white. What am I?

66. If you break me then I am better than I was before, and harder to be broken again. What am I?

67. When you stop and look you can always see me. If you try to touch me you cannot feel me. I cannot move but as you get closer to me I move away. What am I?

68. One way I am a number, reversed I am a snare. What am I?

69. I was was, before was was was.
What am I?

70. Blend a 'teapot shot' so the pearlies won't rot.
What am I?

71. I am the number of letters in the answer to this riddle.
What am I?

72. I walk all day on my head.
What am I?

73. To give me to someone I don't belong is cowardly, but to take me is noble. I can be a game but there are no winners.
Who am I?

74. A father's child, a mother's child but no one's son.
Who am I?

75. You can always find me in the past. I can be created in the present, but the future will never taint me.
What am I?

EASY ANSWERS

1. An upside down centipede

2. A cat

3. A clock

4. Sand

5. An echo

6. Your nose

7. Money

8. An egg

9. A tree

10. Aces

11. Nose

12. *Harvest*

13. *Reflection*

14. *A coin*

15. *Stars*

16. *An iceberg*

17. *Knowledge*

18. *Strawberry*

19. *A chalkboard*

20. *Garbage truck*

21. *A bell*

22. *A peacock*

23. *Your breath*

24. Post Office

25. Darkness

26. Edam

27. A musician

28. A deck of cards

29. Breath

30. Lettuce

31. Light

32. Red paint

33. Mushroom

34. A kangaroo

35. Ohio

36. A hole

37. Boxing ring

38. Not

39. Your brain

40. Your right hand

41. Windows

42. The temperature

43. Time

44. A wedding ring

45. Tomorrow

46. Frost

47. Your voice

48. A ruler

49. Fire

50. Comb

51. A cold

52. The letter 'T'. They are the first letters of one to ten.

53. Your heart

54. Troublesome

55. Infinity

56. An egg

57. Nothing

58. A rainbow

59. The moon

60. *Your name*

61. *A horse*

62. *Water*

63. *An accountant*

64. *A starfish*

65. *A belt*

66. *A violin*

67. *Pawns*

68. *Moose*

69. *Q*

70. *Joke*

71. *Match*

72. Teapot

73. The library

74. Letter O

75. A crown

MEDIUM ANSWERS

1. A breath

2. The letter E

3. A recorder

4. A bar of soap

5. A river

6. A keyhole

7. An eye

8. A clothes hanger

9. A needle

10. A fart

11. A bat

12. The wind

13. A kite

14. An anchor

15. An eagle

16. Windows

17. The ocean

18. A mouse

19. Alphabet

20. A horseman

21. A cloud

22. A heart

23. The riddle teller's son

24. Donut

25. A yard

26. Electricity

27. Water

28. Pea

29. Lounger

30. A worm

31. A compass

32. A pillow

33. A barber

34. Sister

35. A monkey

36. All 5 vowels

37. A windmill

38. A shoe

39. A hurricane

40. Water

41. An alarm clock

42. Skin

43. A telephone

44. An automobile

45. Worm

46. A tongue

47. Carpet

48. Light and darkness

49. Donut

50. A tennis ball

51. A tree

52. A nut

53. Letter 'F'

54. Liver

55. Mars

56. Words

57. Cherry

58. An elevator

59. A taxi driver

60. A snowman

61. Saw

62. Clouds

63. EL

64. D

65. Glasses

66. The moon

67. Screw

68. Fingernails

69. Teeth

70. Bottle

71. Tomorrow

72. *A turtle*

73. *Icicles*

74. *Plate*

75. *0*

DIFFICULT ANSWERS

1. Corn on the cob

2. The brain

3. The pupil

4. Car-pet

5. Paint

6. Mercury thermometer

7. Scissors

8. A beetle

9. A promise

10. Blood

11. Tissue

12. A piano

13. Water (H2O)

14. A golf ball

15. Sawdust

16. Light

17. History

18. A parking lot

19. Light

20. A key

21. A boat

22. A chair

23. Worm

24. Bowling balls

25. A shadow

26. Clouds

27. A feather

28. A sponge

29. Heroine

30. Number 8

31. Fingernails

32. A stapler

33. A goose

34. Grass

35. Tea bag

36. A crane

37. A fish hook

38. Bow

39. Eraser

40. Water

41. Traffic lights

42. Golf

43. Your back

44. Hair

45. Time

46. Elevator

47. A book

48. Words

49. A skull

50. Counterfeit money

51. A snowflake

52. The letter 'J'

53. Music

54. A spiral staircase

55. Weights

56. A grave

57. A teabag

58. Grass

59. The earth

60. A grandfather clock

61. Abbreviation

62. Forgiveness

63. A comet

64. A thimble

65. Dice

66. Imagination

67. Rubber band

68. Ankles

69. Beehive

70. Blank

71. Red herring

72. Human skin

73. Asteroid

74. Body language

75. A secret

FIENDISH ANSWERS

1. A candle

2. Chess pieces

3. A grave stone

4. A seesaw

5. A phone

6. A fish

7. A road

8. A map

9. Gloves

10. Time

11. Mount Rushmore

12. Wheat

13. A broom

14. A snake

15. Zero

16. A dentist

17. Tongs

18. Number 8

19. Die

20. Temper

21. Your mother

22. A clock

23. A drawbridge

24. A shirt

25. Traffic lights

26. A wheelbarrow

27. Tug of war

28. A shirt

29. A water melon

30. David

31. Typewriter

32. Unquestionably

33. A boat

34. Tomorrow is Thursday

35. 78. The numbers are 86-91 upside down.

36. King of Spades

37. A volcano

38. Memory

39. A lock

40. Taking 'n' out of 'window' creates 'widow'. Putting 'n' into 'door' creates 'donor'.

41. Pains

42. A question mark, ?

43. Grape

44. A tornado

45. A pendulum

46. Dice

47. Lamp post

48. Shadow

49. Accelerate

50. Beauty

51. Stable

52. Seesaw

53. SWIMS

54. Sawdust

55. The NATO phonetic alphabet (Tango, golf, hotel India and Juliet)

56. A book

57. A ship

58. Scent, sent and cent

59. A scarecrow

60. A tie

61. Ivy

62. Hourglass

63. Binary

64. Castles

65. Daisy

66. A record

67. Horizon

68. Ten

69. Is

70. Toothpaste – an anagram of teapot shot

71. Four is the only number that fits

72. A nail in a horseshoe

73. Blame

74. A daughter

75. History

Printed in Poland
by Amazon Fulfillment
Poland Sp. z o.o., Wrocław

50988237R00056